D1550496

SRI MRINALINI MATA

President and spiritual head of
Self-Realization Fellowship/Yogoda Satsanga Society of India

How-to-Live Series

SRI MRINALINI MATA

MANIFESTING
DIVINE
CONSCIOUSNESS
— IN —
DAILY LIFE

Self-Realization Fellowship
FOUNDED 1920
Paramahansa Yogananda

ABOUT THIS BOOK: The lectures in *Manifesting Divine Consciousness in Daily Life* were originally published by Self-Realization Fellowship in its quarterly magazine, *Self-Realization,* which was founded by Paramahansa Yogananda in 1925.

Authorized by the International Publications Council of
SELF-REALIZATION FELLOWSHIP
3880 San Rafael Avenue
Los Angeles, California 90065-3219

ISBN-13: 978-0-87612-352-2
ISBN-10: 0-87612-352-3

Printed in the United States of America
1764-J3048

CONTENTS

PREFACE

"Self-realization is the knowing—in body, mind, and soul—that we are one with the omnipresence of God; that we do not have to pray that it come to us, that we are not merely near it at all times, but that God's omnipresence is our omnipresence; that we are just as much a part of Him now as we ever will be. All we have to do is improve our knowing."

—Paramahansa Yogananda

In his "how-to-live" teachings, Paramahansa Yogananda has given to people of all cultures, races, and creeds the means to free themselves from physical, mental, and spiritual inharmonies—to create for themselves a life of enduring happiness and all-round success.

The books in this series present Paramahansaji's how-to-live wisdom on many subjects, providing readers with spiritual insight and practical keys for bringing into daily life the inner balance and harmony that is the essence of yoga. Through the practice of meditation and the universal principles of right action and right attitude highlighted in these books, one can experience every moment as an opportunity to grow in awareness of the Divine.

While each book addresses a distinct topic, one message resonates throughout the series: *Seek God first.* Whether speaking of creating fulfilling relationships, raising spiritual children, overcoming self-defeating habits, or any of the other myriad goals and challenges of modern living, Paramahansa Yogananda again and again refocuses our attention towards life's highest attainment: Self-realization—knowing our true nature as divine beings. Through his inspiration and encouragement, we learn how to live a truly victorious life—transcending limitations, fear, and suffering—by awakening to the infinite power and joy of our real Self: the soul.

— *Self-Realization Fellowship*

Manifesting Divine
Consciousness in Daily Life

PART I

Practical Lessons in Manifesting Divine Consciousness in Daily Life

Condensed from a talk given by Mrinalini Mata in Auckland during a visit to SRF centers in Australia and New Zealand

It is such a privilege to be here in your beautiful country, and to greet all of you, Gurudeva Paramahansa Yogananda's disciples, halfway around the world. No matter what the locale, no matter what the nationality, every individual who is following these teachings is part of one fellowship of souls seeking God. As our Guru often said to us, "All of you devotees are as my family. And even after I am gone, there are many, many devotees yet to come, from the far corners of the world. I know who they are, and they will be drawn by God to seek Him. They will feel a great divine awakening and love, which will bring them to this path for the fulfillment of that realization." The one wish in my heart, my deep prayer, is to bring to you — and to leave in your hearts, minds, and souls — a deeper longing for God, and a deeper awareness of the reality of His presence, the nearness to each one of us of that Infinite Being.

Those of us blessed to be around Paramahansaji found in him a living embodiment of all the spiritual ideals, all the spiritual goals, that our hearts had ever yearned for — all that we had ever imagined in our deepest probing thoughts about the Infinite. During our years of receiving his guidance and training in the ashram, we came to understand what it really means to seek God and to know God. I am sure most of us found our preconceptions about the spiritual life changed as the years went on. We saw that seeking God does not mean a negation of life. It is rather, and has ever been, the most practical of human endeavors. The devotee who draws closer and closer to God does not become a withdrawn or strange human being. On the contrary, as one begins to feel the unity of the soul with God, he or she becomes the most balanced of individuals.

Nor does it mean experiencing miracles or accumulating miraculous powers. Often when people begin to think of seeking God or following a guru, it is with expectations of phenomenal displays and happenings. Humanity for the most part lives only on the surface of life. They are concentrated on material existence, and that is as far as their thinking goes — desires for, and attachments to, the outer forms: "I must have this and that in order to live, to survive, to raise my family." So in terms of seeking God, the attitude tends to be: "Lord, I am seeking You now; therefore, let my life be filled with miracles. Let all my troubles dissolve, all my sorrows disappear. When I pray to You, give me Your instant answer and heal this body of the diseases and sufferings of life. When I come to a guru, a spiritual teacher, I want to see him perform the miracles that I have read about in the Bible and the scriptures."

When Master's guru and *paramgurus*,* at the behest of God, first sent him to the West

---

* "Master" is a respectful title often used by disciples when referring to Paramahansa Yogananda — one who had attained self-mastery. It serves as an English equivalent for "Guru," the customary Sanskrit term for one's spiritual preceptor.

A *paramguru* is the guru of one's guru. Here, the term *paramgurus* refers to the line of SRF gurus — Sri Yukteswar, Lahiri Mahasaya, and Mahavatar to bring the teachings of Yoga, he used to give public demonstrations of the power of God, the infinite potential of the mind and will, just as Christ did in his day. But he told us later: "People would ask for healing for the body; or they asked me to pray for success in their business. But after their bodies were healed or they found their business improving, they forgot all about God. They stayed on the surface, never seeking something deeper." In later years, therefore, he ceased giving such demonstrations. He wanted to concentrate on the real ideal of his mission, and that was to awaken in each receptive heart a deep love and longing for God, so that God would become the Primary Reality in the life of each one.

Often when devotees ask, "Tell us stories about Master," they expect to hear tales of

---

Babaji — whose Christlike lives are described in Paramahansa Yogananda's *Autobiography of a Yogi.*

miraculous healings and powers. Master had these powers; I saw him demonstrate them many times. But I came to know this: The power of that Guru was so much deeper, so much greater than any phenomenal display. He had the power to uplift and permanently transform the lives of human beings.

Think of the many hundreds, perhaps thousands, who in Jesus Christ's lifetime saw the miraculous powers of God that he demonstrated. How many of those thousands were with Christ at the cross? How many were changed, were truly transformed in spirit — so that at the hour of Christ's suffering, they could stand at the cross with him whose own love for God was so deep that he could take all the tests, all the suffering of betrayal and crucifixion? There were only a few. Most people turn aside from the spiritual path when it comes to the real "getting down to business" of knowing and finding and securing God in their lives.

The greatest miracle that any teacher or prophet can perform is to take a human being who is bound up in the delusions of *maya,* in the self-centered desires and attachments and the confusions of this world, and to touch that soul with a love for God that will give true meaning, a worthwhile goal, a divine purpose to his or her life.

THE TRUE MEANING OF RELIGION

If you could have been in the physical presence of our own blessed Guru, you would have seen that the most phenomenal power he demonstrated was this: the divine love for God, and the divine love coming from God, that flowed through his eyes and through his whole being. I saw how that love changed my own life and the lives of all of us around him. It made God the most real and the most important thing to us in this world. And I see, even today, how that transformation takes place in the lives of every seeker who truly follows his teachings and thereby comes within the aura of his ever-living presence and consciousness.

Gurudeva came to the West with a special divine dispensation, received from Christ and the Great Ones: to bring the life back into religion, to reawaken the true meaning of religion. Instead of outward "churchianity," as he called it, he taught how to build a temple within ourselves, where daily we enter to meditate deeply on God, where daily we live to serve Him. Religion, he taught, must be an actual experience of God, not just words or scriptural precepts. "I do not ask you to believe blindly," he would say. "I do not ask you to accept any dogma. But I say this to you: if you practice and apply these teachings and meditation techniques, you will realize within your own self the presence of God and the truth of the words I speak to you."

So in talking tonight about our Guru, I want to dwell on his practicality — the actual practices he taught that bring God into one's life. In our training he began with the very basics of the spiritual path. It is said in the Indian scriptures that the essential purpose of religion is to elevate humanity to a consciousness of Bliss (which is God) by removing man's threefold suffering — physical, mental, and spiritual — by the roots, so there is no chance of recurrence.

To remove this suffering, one must understand its causes. All suffering and misunderstanding, all our separation from God, is a result of *maya,* cosmic delusion — which manifests in the individual as ignorance. If we would know God, if we would pursue a path that will bring us to that high state of consciousness beyond all suffering, then we must know how to remove ignorance of our true nature: divine souls—immortal, blissful, free.

In this physical body, and with this physically limited mind, ignorance takes many forms. It has many offshoots, and it is very, very subtle. If we were to break it down and analyze how to overcome it, we would come to the very teachings our Guru imparted to us through everyday life in the ashram. And these are applicable to all, whether they live in the world or in a monastery.

TRANSCENDING THE LIKES AND DISLIKES OF THE EGO

One form of ignorance that afflicts the consciousness of most persons is being a slave to likes and dislikes. Do we realize how much they govern our lives? So much of what we do is motivated not by understanding of what is right or wrong, but by irrational feelings of attraction or repulsion within us. A primary tenet of a spiritual life is learning to rise above these likes and dislikes of the body-identified ego, to allow expression of the higher discrimination of the soul.

This does not mean a negation of life, or that you cease to enjoy things. It means you cease to be bound by the habits created by likes and dislikes, which perpetuate in you the delusion of being a limited, mortal human being.

"You must remember," Master would say to us, "that you are made in the image of God. But is the image of God this little body and mind and five senses, which are so limited and experience comparatively so little? No. The image of God in us is the soul. The human mind and body are only outer instruments through which the soul expresses. You will always be bound by ignorance and limited by the body and the senses if you allow them to dictate to you: 'I like this, and therefore I do this. I don't like that, therefore I won't do that.'"

I'll give you a simple illustration of how he taught us. There is a food in India, a very healthful food called bitter squash, *karela*. Master was very fond of it, as I've found that most Hindus are, and he often had it served in the ashram. It was difficult for me to like it. But knowing that we are not supposed to have likes and dislikes, I never expressed this to Master.

One day as we were eating with him in the dining room of the Encinitas Hermitage, he was serving this bitter squash. I was not feeling well that day. I had a painful stomach-ache. So I thought, "Well, this is a good excuse. Today I don't have to eat it. I will simply tell Master that I am not well, and therefore I will be excused." So when he started to hand some food to me, I declined. I said, "I have a very severe stomachache. I'd rather not eat this."

He said, "Oh, you have a stomachache?"

"Yes, Master."

He said, "Never mind, come here." So I rose from my chair and went over to him. He took my hands in his, and he said, "Now look at me; look me in the eye. Take a deep breath. Now exhale. Stomachache is gone, isn't it?" And it was — instantaneously.

"Yes, Guru."

He said, "Eat. Here — dig in!"

But that was not the end of the bitter squash lesson! Sometime later he was serving it again, and I guess I felt very bold that day. He started to give me a big helping, and I said, "Master, just give me a little bit. I don't like that bitter squash."

"Oh?" he said. "You don't like it?"

"No, Master."

He called one of the disciples to bring a large bowl. Then Master took the whole serving plate of bitter squash and put it in that bowl. He handed it to me and said, "Sit down and eat." I had to sit there and eat the whole bowl of bitter squash.

The lessons Master gave us were simple and direct, and they had a wonderfully freeing effect on us. We soon learned that anything he said to us — even seemingly casual directions or the most rudimentary instruction — was important. We found that in each instance, in all of his interactions with us, he was working to root out the offshoots of ignorance, which often are buried deep within our consciousness. He dealt not so much with what we were saying, but with our thoughts, the level of consciousness our being was dwelling on. Step by step, he guided us on our way toward divine expansion and freedom.

I never again said to Guruji that I did not like something! I learned, as we all did, to keep the emotions and the feelings under control. Our soul's discrimination must always be the master of our thoughts and feelings and desires. You can learn this by starting with the "bitter squashes" in your own life. Encourage yourself to do little things that you ought to but don't like to do, and do them with the consciousness, "This is not so bad after all. This is good for me." Begin with small things, and you will find how, little by little, your soul becomes more free.

AWAKENING THE SOUL'S DIVINE POWER OF WILL

Another one of the root causes of suffering, which allows ignorance to govern one's life, is lack of will power, not using the divinely given will that is present in every soul. Our Guru emphasized not only will power to do what you ought to do, but he also coined the phrase "won't power" — the power to prevent yourself from doing those things that you should not do. He taught (and demonstrated in his own life) that each human being, being made in the image of God, has within him or her a spark of the infinite will of God. We can do anything that we put our minds to if we are attuned to that will of the Divine.

So, in addition to "I like this" and "I don't like that," two other words that Master never allowed us to say were: "I can't." Whenever he asked us to do something, he never said, "Do you know how to do this?" or, "Can you do this?" He would simply assign a task to us and say, "You do this." And our answer was always, "Yes, Master." Then it was up to us to find out how we would get it done.

There were many ways in which he taught us to develop will power. I was still going to school when I met Master, and I finished the last three years of my schooling at a public school in Encinitas while living in the ashram. It was difficult for me because I wanted to stay with Master, to serve him throughout the day. At that time he was traveling back and forth frequently between Mt. Washington and Encinitas to speak in our temples in San Diego and Los Angeles, and I wanted to be able to travel with him — but no, I had to go to school. There were a number of us devotees in school at that time, and he expected all of us to strive for the highest grades in our classes. He used to say that if people in the world can have the ambition to reach the top, why shouldn't those who love God express in their lives the highest ideals, the highest achievements. "Whatever is worth doing is worth doing well," he told us.

One time, Gurudeva was inviting the devotees in the ashram in Encinitas to come to Los Angeles to attend some big function there.

Then he turned to me and said, "But you have your exams starting the next day. These are very important. You must stay home and study."

I was brokenhearted. I said, "But Master, please let me go. If you do, then after this function is over, I promise you I will stay up all night to study. When we drive back to Encinitas in the morning, I will go directly to school. But I will spend the whole night studying."

Master looked at me for a moment, and then said, "All right. You may come." So we went to Los Angeles and attended the function in the city, then drove to the Mother Center. It was very late when we reached there, at least one o'clock. I went to my room upstairs. Master stayed downstairs, talking with some of the monks. I knew that if I sat down I would fall asleep. I thought, "No, I have promised Master that I would spend this night studying for my exam." So I stood up. I leaned against the wall, with the book in my hand, studying.

It must have been about three a.m. when Master came upstairs. He knocked on the door, and when he opened it, he saw me standing there studying. He said to me, "Oh, poor thing, it's so late, you need your rest. Why don't you retire now? You retire and get some rest."

I thought, "How nice. Master is going to relieve me of that promise to him." Then I thought, "Well, I must do my part. I mustn't give in too easily; I must assure him that I am willing to fulfill my promise."

"No, Master," I said, "I promised you that I would spend the rest of the night staying up and studying if you would let me come." I was thinking, "Surely he's going to say now, 'No, that's all right; you get some rest now.'" He just looked at me and said, "That's good." He closed the door and left me.

I spent the rest of the night going over my schoolwork very conscientiously. The next day when I took the exam, through Master's blessings and my own efforts, my will, I received the highest grade in the class.

In these ways, Guruji trained us not to give in to the human frailties of the body. If he saw us ever becoming lax, he would pointedly remark, "What is this?!" in that tone of voice which immediately set us straight! It was to remind us of what he taught: "Within your little finger, you have enough energy — atomic, electrical, divine energy — if it could be released, to run the city of Chicago for three days. And you say that you are tired? Or that you can't do this and you can't do that? The will is the dynamo that draws on this energy, this infinite potential of God within you."

Master himself was indefatigable. He never seemed to tire. He served without thought of the body, all hours of the day and night. He didn't know time. The most we ever saw him give rest to his body was three or four hours at night. Even during that time, he was not sleeping in the ordinary way. He would say, "You think that I go to bed and sleep. But I am lifted up in the Infinite Consciousness."

We who were serving with Master had to serve at the same pace. It was a great exercise of our will. Sometimes we would serve twenty hours a day, or even around the clock. It was a wonderful demonstration in our lives of how the power of God sustains the body and the mind of one who serves with willingness and with the consciousness of His presence.

One does not have to live in an ashram to apply this principle. Wherever one is, one's life can be infused with that consciousness: "From God I have come. It is by the direct power of God that I live. My will, my life, my vitality, is but a minute borrowing of that infinite power of God. Therefore, I think of Him, I remember Him, throughout the performance of all life's duties, accomplishing whatever the circumstances of my life require. I recognize that infinite power of God within me and flowing through me, breathing through my breath, serving through my hands, thinking through my thoughts. And ultimately into that infinite God I will melt again after this little mortal body has fulfilled its part in life."

Through all these lessons, the Guru was teaching us: Learn to awaken the divine power that is within you to help you overcome the delusive suggestion of ignorance or limitation, which says, "I am this little body; I feel this pain, I feel this sickness. My body cannot do this because it is suffering. My body has to have warm clothing because it is cold. My body has to have a certain kind of food because I have a problem in my stomach." Remember, the mind and the will are the seat of the power of God within you. Exercise that divine power. Make it stronger and stronger by using it, and you will see how real it becomes in your life.

EVENMINDEDNESS: OVERCOMING THE POWER OF MAYA'S DUALITIES

Another way in which *maya,* cosmic delusion, keeps us in ignorance of our divine nature, identified with the physical body and its limitations, is through the ceaselessly alternating dualities of life. This whole creation is based on the principle of relativity, or duality — positive and negative; joy contrasting with sorrow, pleasure with pain, light with shadow, life with death. In the consciousness of one who identifies with the physical world, the experience of these opposites creates a disturbance of the thoughts and emotions. The scriptures teach that God's presence is reflected in each of us as the soul, our true Self; and our Guru often gave this illustration: "A reflection of the moon appears distorted in a wind-ruffled lake; similarly, the reflected soul-image in the body is not clearly seen in a restless, sense-identified mind." In order to fully reflect the image of God, the lake of one's consciousness must be perfectly still, unruffled by the storms of life, the constant changes of dualities and relativities.

Meditation, of course, is essential for attaining that inner stillness.* And, the Bhagavad Gita teaches, the only way to perceive God while outwardly engaged in life is by

---

* "When by meditation techniques we withdraw restless thoughts from the lake of the mind, we behold our soul, a perfect reflection of Spirit, and realize that the soul and God are One." — *Paramahansa Yogananda*

practicing evenmindedness. That means keeping the lake of our consciousness undisturbed by emotions in the face of life's inevitable dualities. This does not make us become automatons, with no feeling. I know of no human being who expressed such enjoyment of life, such deep feelings of divine love and compassion, as our Guru. He felt deeply the joys and sorrows of life; but he used to say, "Even when I am experiencing these things on the outside, my mind always maintains the still clearness in which the image of God and my consciousness reflect as one perfect being."

Most people do not realize how they constantly limit their happiness and freedom by overreacting to the contrasts of duality encountered in daily life. For example, heat and cold — how very susceptible the body is to extremes of temperature! Yogis in India test their power of evenmindedness by enduring extremes of either heat or cold without letting the consciousness become disturbed; and Master often made us practice this in the ashram.

In the later years of his life Guruji spent much time at his retreat in the desert, working on his writings. It was there that he did most of his Bhagavad Gita translation and commentary.* He would dictate, and one of us would sit at the typewriter and take down his words. Sometimes he worked for many, many hours at a time — all day, and usually late into the night.

There was a little fenced-in compound around this desert retreat, and after Master was through with his work, he would say, "Come now, let us walk around the compound, under the stars and the moon." It can

---

* *God Talks With Arjuna: The Bhagavad Gita — Royal Science of God-Realization* (published by Self-Realization Fellowship).

be very cold in the desert at night, well below freezing. There was one period when it was exceptionally cold, bitterly so; and living in southern California we didn't have much winter clothing. One night we went out about three o'clock in the morning to walk. I had on a coat, and I had taken a blanket and wrapped it around me. Master was wearing just a little jacket. He was walking, inhaling the fresh air, feeling wonderful; but I was shivering miserably! It was so cold I could hardly walk! Finally, after going around the compound a couple of times, I thought, "Well, surely this is enough." I saw that he was starting around again, and I said, "Master, it's so cold, would you excuse me? I'd like to go inside."

"Cold?!" he said. "Look at me; I'm not cold. Why do you allow your mind to accept the idea of cold?"

Well, it was already suggested to my mind by then, so I had a difficult time changing. I continued to feel frozen for the rest of that walk around the compound.

The next evening I remembered that lesson, and I thought, "Master wasn't cold. He said it is all in the mind; therefore, I say to my mind, *It is not cold.*" But I was tempted: I looked at the thermometer as we walked out the back door. It was colder than it had been the night before — and the wind chill made it worse, because the wind was blowing so strongly you could hardly walk against it. But this time I had conditioned my mind. I affirmed, "No, it isn't cold. I am going to enjoy this experience. I am going to think of God, and the beauty of the heavens, the stars, and the moon, in the presence of my Guru."

We walked outside for almost an hour that night, and I didn't feel cold at all. Just that simple suggestion to the mind made the difference. So it works. I know it works. If I can do it, you all can do it. Learn to suggest positive thoughts to your mind. Suggest them strongly. Believe in them when you suggest them, and you will see what miracles they work in your life. You will see how you become master of the body and of the mind.

Guruji, being very practical, used to say: "If you are cold and there is a heater available, turn it on — or put on an overcoat! If you are hot, and you can turn on the fan, do so. But never allow the mind to become ruffled, upset, or unhappy if you cannot change these conditions."

MIND POWER AND RIGHT ATTITUDE IN THE FACE OF PAIN

The yogi must also learn to maintain even-mindedness when dealing with sickness and bodily suffering. This is perhaps one of the most difficult tests, because when there is pain

in the body, it is hard to practice the philoso-
phy that matter is unreal, or to realize "I am
not the body." At that moment you feel very
much identified with the physical form!

Master demonstrated for us how one
should react to suffering and pain in the
physical form — maintaining unruffled even-
mindedness and an attitude of surrender to
and faith in God, while constantly making the
effort to exert the power of mind over matter,
of mind over pain.

It is said that great saints and mas-
ters — those who have reunited themselves
with God — have the ability to take on the
karmic effects of the wrong actions of others,
and to work them out on their own bodies.
This can be compared to the situation of a
very weak person who is about to be hit by a
very strong person. If another strong individual steps in front of the weak person, he can
endure the blow. It does not affect him much,

whereas it might have been death-dealing to the weak person.

Our own Guru has this ability to help other souls and alleviate their burdens. I saw him do so many times; and he himself told us, "I have taken the karma of you all, and of so many." Devotees from all over the world would write to him and ask him for healing. I can remember him reading these letters in the early mornings. He would sit on his chair, cross-legged in meditation, and would pray deeply for each one. During such times we occasionally saw manifested in minor ways on Master's own body some symptoms of an illness that he had taken, by the grace and power of God, from an individual who had sought his help.

Toward the end of his life, Master told us that God had warned him he had already taken onto his body too much karma from others. "Divine Mother is telling me that I must not take any more," he said. But I never saw him refuse anyone. He couldn't.

Guruji not only absorbed karma of individuals who sought his help; he also had the power to absorb what is called mass karma.* Very great souls can do this; that is why John the Baptist could say of Jesus that he "taketh away the sin of the world." For example, during the Korean War which began in 1950, sometimes we would be with Gurudeva and hear his words during profound states of *samadhi* when he would cry out in pain as he felt the machine gun bullets in his own body,

---

* "The combined karma of groups of individuals — social or racial groups, or nations, for example — or of the world at large, constitute the mass karma of the earth or portions thereof....A store of good mass karma from living in harmony with divine laws and forces blesses man's earthly environment with peace, health, prosperity. Accumulated bad mass karma precipitates wars, diseases, poverty, devastating earthquakes, and other such calamities." — *Paramahansa Yogananda*

and the suffering of those boys who were dying on the far-off battlefield. He went through similar experiences during World War II — as well as in the late 1940s when in India there were great floods and famine and starvation. In his *samadhi*-oneness with afflicted humanity, he experienced in his own form the agonies of that suffering as God allowed him to absorb much of the burden of mass karma in order to alleviate the pain and darkness of mankind.

WITNESSING THE DIVINE CONSCIOUSNESS BY WHICH SUFFERING CAN BE TRANSCENDED

I remember at the time of our first World Convocation, held at the Mother Center in 1950, Master was having a particular difficulty with his legs. He was not even able to stand or walk without the most extreme pain, so it was arranged that he would be driven in a car down to the tennis court where the gathering was to be held. We were all praying, and worrying, "How will he ever be able to get up onto the platform to give his talk?" As the car drove up and stopped, those of us who knew the difficulties his body was going through at that time were holding our breath anxiously. The door opened and Master stepped out of the car — and we all gasped in unison, because it really seemed that Master did not walk but floated, his feet barely touching the ground, as he made his way up the ramp to the podium.

He stood there for two hours and spoke to the people; and then he greeted everyone who had come — staying for many, many hours after his talk. Afterward, when he returned to his rooms, he said to us all: "This has been one of the greatest experiences of my life. See how Divine Mother shows you the unreality of life and its alternating contrasts! On one side, you see how this body suffered; on this other side you see I am completely aloof. I am held in the arms of Divine Mother; and I don't know this body or its suffering at all."

Guruji used to say to us: "My life has two sides, like the two sides of a coin." On one side he was always aware that all creation — his body, our bodies, this room, this table, this chair, everything — is made of that infinite Divine Consciousness in which there are no limitations, no pain or suffering. It is only the suggestion of God which is imposed upon creation (*maya*) that divides the Infinite into seemingly separate finite forms and makes them seem real. Master used to call it a cosmic hypnosis. God is suggesting the reality of this world and of this body to us, and because of this hypnotic thought powerfully suggested by God, we accept them as real.

Guruji explained to us that in taking on a physical body, even avatars — those great souls who have already attained liberation but who return to earth, as did our Guru, to help free others, to help free the world, to show seeking souls the way to find God — even they have to take on a certain amount of delusion or limitation. Without that delusion, without the *maya* that seems to make this world real, the very atoms of their body could not stay together. They would be as they truly are: nothing but the unconditioned light and consciousness of God.

We saw this in the life of our Guru — how he was living in a physical body like yours and mine, which was capable of feeling pain and was subject to the limitations of illness and injury; and how at the same time he could express the infinite power and potential of the mind to transcend those physical "realities." When he said to the body, "Get up and walk," even if it was sick or suffering, that body got up and walked. Sometimes it would seem impossible that he would be able to fulfill a lecture engagement, or to meet with people who had come from far away to see him. Undaunted, he would prepare for the meeting or interview, and when the time came, suddenly all trace of the ailment would leave. Because of his exertion of will, and because of his faith in that Infinite Power within him, as he said, "God always comes to my aid. Divine Mother never tells me up to the last moment whether or not She is going to give me the power and the ability, whether or not She is going to remove these tests, the suffering, from me. All I know is that it is now time to serve Her, to share God with these who have come seeking my help. But always at the last moment, it is as though She lifts me up in Her arms, into that great Love and that great Light."

So he told us after that occasion at Convocation: "When I stepped from the car, suddenly I no longer had the consciousness or the feeling of the body. The body, and all of the people and surroundings, just became one mass of the light of God. And I felt myself floating in that light, that consciousness of God." We who were there saw it — it was a real miracle that we witnessed. And we knew that a divine power had elevated our Guru at that moment.

"THE ONLY HAVEN OF SAFETY"

"On one side of my consciousness," Guruji would say, "there is the material world and body. Yet always — even when I am expressing through this physical form — always on the other side I see the unreality of it all."

One time at the desert, he had been dictating his Bhagavad Gita interpretations. We were sitting at his feet, and he was discussing some very deep ideas about the nature of creation, and the unreality of this world — how God imposes His *maya* on humankind, making us think that this is all so real and so important. Then he became very withdrawn for a time. There was a certain look that came over Master's countenance when his consciousness became deeply internalized and focused upon God. We always recognized that expression and would become silent.

As we sat there waiting for him to resume working, suddenly he began to laugh! Master had a wonderfully hearty and very contagious laugh, and soon we were all laughing with him. Finally he said, "Oh, it is such a joke! It is such a trick that God is playing on you all! How unreal this world and its experiences are. It is all God; it is all God's movie — the play of God's light and shadow in this movie house of the cosmos. It is not real; it is not real! Divine Mother is just fooling you! You take it so seriously, but it is just a joke Divine Mother is having with you!"

But then he became very serious, and tears of divine compassion began rolling down his cheeks as he looked around at each one of us. "But I feel so sorry for all of you," he said with great tenderness, "because to you this world is yet real."

"Don't take it too seriously," he went on. "Just see it all as a show of God — its joys and sorrows, its disappointments, its delusions, its pains, life and death. A good movie has all of those things! Whenever circumstances begin to disturb you, to pull you down and make you feel discouraged, turn your thoughts to God and say, 'Oh, but I know, Lord, this is only a temporary dream-movie projected by the beam of Your light and consciousness. I am a spark of that infinite light and consciousness playing for a time a little human role in this body, and I know it is not real.' Learn to laugh at the show that God is tricking you into thinking is real. Learn to see the Reality behind the movie scenes of delusion. Look to Divine Mother. Look to the beam. That is the only haven of safety."

RISING ABOVE THE EGO'S MOODS

Another of the roots of ignorance embedded in our "second nature" or ego — keeping our consciousness limited to duality — are the alternating moods of happiness and sorrow. These also are part of the delusion that we must learn to transcend. I remember one morning when Master called for me. I was just bubbling with happiness that day. But the minute I stepped into his room, Master began to scold me. Some of the things he was scolding me for were not my responsibility or my fault; but even so, his scolding was so severe that my joy vanished. It just drained right out of me, and I began to feel extremely sad. After a few minutes, he sent me back to my duties.

We had learned that Master always had a reason for whatever training he gave to us. We did not try to defend ourselves, or to explain or justify our actions, because we knew that he was not dealing only with what we were thinking or doing at the moment. He was digging deep into the soil of our consciousness, trying to remove all seeds of imperfections that were lodged within and to bring out the perfection of God hidden in our souls.

I began thinking, "Well now, I deserved that scolding. Whether it was merited for the particular things I was being scolded for or not does not matter. I must always accept these things with the right attitude." Little by little, my peace and my attunement with Master began to come back. And the moment it did, he called me to him again.

This time he was all love and kindness, which is how we usually found him. "You see how you came in to me this morning," he said, "and you were all smiles, all happy? And then with just a little pinprick of scolding, how that faded away? You must learn to cultivate the joy of God in the wintertime of life, when there are trials and troubles, as well as in the summertime, when everything is going beautifully for you. If you don't learn to do this, then in that time of trial, when some little disturbance comes into your life, your joy will ebb away — and you will find that in losing that joy, you lose also the consciousness of God. When I scolded you this morning, your happiness should not have dried up as it did. You should have been able to hold on to that happiness — in the wintertime of trouble as well as in the summertime of peace and satisfaction and ease of contentment."

These experiences with Master, these simple but deeply meaningful lessons, we never forgot; and we learned how to apply them to each circumstance of our lives. We saw, for example, that when a devotee is too much swayed or influenced by the alternating waves of joy and sorrow that agitate the consciousness of most human beings, the result is moodiness.

Moods, our Guru used to say, are an expression of bad karma from the past — wrong tendencies or desires that we have not spiritually overcome, but are not allowing to come out in this lifetime. In other words, we have now learned that certain actions are wrong, that we should not engage in them. So we put up a mental barrier and say, "I will not do this." But if the seed of that action is still within the consciousness, then even if one thwarts its direct expression, it may very well come out in the form of moods.

You may be quite happy one minute, and then for no rational cause your mood becomes depressed, discouraged. Some little occurrence — completely out of proportion to your reaction — makes you feel as if all of your will and enthusiasm is gone and you begin to feel extremely sorry for yourself: "Oh, life treats me so unfairly! All the good fortune and blessings seem to come into the lives of others. I never get a break!" Such moods are confining, suffocating to the spirit. Master never allowed us to indulge in them — and he always knew when we were in one!

In my early years on the path I was subject to moods, but Master's strict discipline and God's blessing enabled me to overcome this. I remember one day I was in a depressed mood when he summoned several of us to come to his room. The others were already there when I arrived, and he was meditating, his eyes closed. He didn't open his eyes to see me, but the moment I came to the door, he waved his hand to dismiss me and said, "Mrina, don't come into my room! Don't come around me with those negative vibrations. Go back to your room!"

I returned to my room — and then I was really upset! I thought, "Here I was feeling so lonely and discouraged — longing to be a perfect devotee of God, and feeling self-pity that I was so far from that goal. All I needed from Master was just a word of encouragement, and my mood would have been gone. If he had just said, 'Oh, you are doing fine. I will help you. Just keep on meditating, ever more deeply....' Just a little love and encouragement — that's all I needed. But now, instead of helping me, he sent me away!"

We soon learned that this was Master's way of training us. Whenever we were out of attunement with Master, he banished us from his presence. This is a very important point for all of you to understand who did not have the opportunity to be in the Guru's physical presence. Even when he was with us physically, he disciplined and guided us not so much through personal contact and communication on a material level as by spiritual attunement. If our spiritual attunement was right with Master, then we were able to receive and benefit from his help and blessings — and outwardly he allowed us around him. But if our spiritual attunement was a little off, Master shut the door on us; he sent us away.

When that happened, there was only one thing to do. We would go to our rooms, feeling so unhappy. Where were we to turn? We would get on our knees before God, before our altar, and we would cry and pray to God, "Show me where I am wrong. Change me. Give me attunement with my Guru. Give me attunement with You. Change this gross mortal form, with all of its imperfections and limitations, into an instrument through which You can live and express in this world for the good of self and of all humankind, of all the world."

As we prayed in this way, suddenly we would feel a great peace: We had lifted our consciousness from the disturbing moods, limitations, and delusion of the ego, and had brought it back to stillness, to attunement with God and Master. The moment that peace returned — invariably I saw this happen — there would come a knock on the door, or someone would slip a little note under the door saying, "Master would like to see you now."

When we then went to his room, he was again all love and joy. He would say, "Well, well! I should not have scolded you that

way. You didn't deserve such scolding. I am
so sorry that I caused you pain." We would
just bow to Master and say, "Oh, Master,
give me that discipline any time, all of the
time!" With attunement came understanding: His scolding was a blessing, given because he cared enough to shake us out of
the delusions of limitation of the body and
mind.

Today, although I no longer have that
physical contact with him, I see that the
guidance and blessing coming from our
Guru is just as real as it was during his lifetime. I know when he is disciplining or
guiding me. It is just as tangible, and it can
be just as painful! But that guidance and
that pain help me to overcome. Similarly in
the lives of each of you who is sincerely
seeking God, you will find that the Guru
helps and guides you on your way. As you
do your part on the spiritual path, you will

receive his blessings; and through those blessings and your own efforts, you will receive the blessings and grace of God.

God and Guru will send tests; They will discipline you when you need it. But you learn as you continue on the path — just as we had to learn, and are still constantly learning — to accept that discipline with the right attitude. You realize with every joy and every sorrow that comes to you that this is not just a chance circumstance. It is coming to you from God and Guru, as part of your karma that you are ready to work out at that time, and it comes for a reason. There is a lesson in it for you to learn. Once you learn it, you will find that you are that much freer, that much closer to God. You will be a little less confined to the limitations of this body and this mind; and you will feel that Infinite Power, that Infinite

Love and Joy, expressing just a little more in your life.

ANCHORING THE CONSCIOUSNESS IN THE DIVINE

Master taught us that one of the major causes of ignorance — forgetfulness of our divine nature — is the constant barrage of distractions in this world, which disturb the consciousness and draw the attention outward. The mind is continually being made to think of other things and to forget God, whereas the devotee who would have God-realization must learn to anchor the consciousness and the thoughts constantly in the Divine.

Master trained us to do this in many ways. Sometimes we would come to his rooms, our minds very much filled with work matters — decisions that we needed him to make, projects that he had asked us to work on, and so forth. We would be full of enthusiasm for getting things done, all immersed in business and activity consciousness. He would give his attention to these matters for a time and then — right in the midst of it all, when our minds were busy trying to solve the many problems inherent in running an organization — he would suddenly say, "All right, now sit down and let's meditate."

We would sit for meditation; and if our minds were at all restless, Master knew it. He would say: "Is your love for God so little, so stale, that you cannot keep your mind from wandering and being attracted by these restless thoughts? Pinpoint the mind on God. Drop the thought of anything else and plunge the whole consciousness into God." So we learned to do that. Then after a period of meditation, Master would say, "All right now, go back to work." Instantaneously we had to change our consciousness and resume our duties — with the same enthusiasm, the same attention, the same concentration — picking up right where we had left off.

"This is the way the true yogi, the true devotee, goes through life," Master told us. "The ordinary person is like a pendulum, swinging back and forth from one extreme to another, always moving, always restless. The yogi, on the other hand, is always calm, centered in his true nature, like a stilled pendulum."

"The peaceful person remains calm until he is ready to work; then he swings into action," Guruji said. "As soon as he is through, he swings back to the center of calmness. You should always be calm, like the pendulum that is still, but ready to swing into steady action whenever necessary." And then he took it a step further: After we left meditation, we were to carry with us into our duties and activities that consciousness of meditation — the consciousness of doing everything as service to God, with His power, His energy, His vitality flowing through us.

MEDITATION IS THE GREATEST WAY TO FREE THE SOUL

In this *satsanga,* I have shared some of the very practical ways taught by Guruji through which you can free the soul from ignorance, from all that binds it to mortal consciousness — methods that you can practice in the world just as we practice them in the ashram. Through them, you will more and more begin to realize the ultimate truth: "I am not this body. I am the soul, one with the Infinite Spirit."

The greatest method of all for reaching and maintaining that consciousness is to follow the spiritual instruction of the Guru on deep meditation. Through meditation, you quiet the thoughts and the consciousness and let them rest like that stilled pendulum — centered in God, in the stillness where you begin to perceive His presence.

Master stressed that we should make each moment of meditation count, each moment a communion with God, a communion of our whole being with that Reality. Once a few of us were with him when he took a period of seclusion in Arizona to work on his writings. Our days were very busy, and one morning I made a special effort to waken myself earlier, before I thought Master would call me, so that I could have a little more time for meditation. It wasn't a very deep meditation, but still I was proud of myself for meditating longer that morning. However, when I saw Master, he looked at me and said, "You didn't meditate this morning."

I protested, "But Master, I meditated a whole hour."

He replied: "Half an hour should have been enough."

My spiritual pride was crushed! But I pondered this for a while; then understanding came, and I knew what he was saying: "You meditated an hour, meaning you sat in the meditation posture for an hour, but if you had meditated even half of that time with depth and intensity, you would have gotten twice as much result from your meditation."

I recall also one of the monks, when he met Master in the hallway, very proudly saying to him, "Master, this morning I did three hundred Kriyas" — thinking that Master was going to say, "Oh, you blessed *chela*, how wonderful; I'm so proud of you!" But Master just kept walking down the hallway, saying very nonchalantly as he passed:

"Three should have been enough." That is how he stressed the importance of depth in meditation.

EVEN A BRIEF GLIMPSE OF DIVINE CONSCIOUSNESS TRANSFORMS ONE'S LIFE

Any person who has truly experienced even a brief glimpse of God can never again be the same — can never again be satisfied with limited worldly consciousness as before. You do not cease to enjoy the world or its wholesome pleasures; there is just a turning of the awareness from the outer side to the inner side of reality. Instead of being identified with physical forms and limitations, attachments and desires, likes and dislikes, joys and sorrows, you see all of life as an expression of God. You perceive everything as made out of His infinite light and consciousness. You enjoy the love and companionship of your family because you feel flowing through you His love, which He has given you to love that family. In the love you in turn receive from them, you feel not just a selfish, physical, limited human emotion but that infinite love of the Divine. When you look at a rose, or the myriad beautiful things that God has created, you see behind the beauty of the petals the infinite light and consciousness of the Creator who has made and who sustains that beauty.

As Master reminded us: The real devotee is not one who is always saying, "When will I find God? Where is He? I long for God; how shall I be able to find Him?" The real devotee is that soul who says, "Ah! I have God. He is all the time with me, within me, around me. I know it is God who is loving me through the forms of all my loved ones, that it is He who is the beauty behind the rose and the sunset; that it is His power and life which is beating in my heart and flowing through my breath. I am a part of Him, every moment of every day."

Learn to think that way. As Lord Krishna tells Arjuna in the Bhagavad Gita, learn to anchor your consciousness in That which is changeless — so that, in our Guru's words, you can "stand unshaken midst the crash of breaking worlds." No matter what experiences you go through externally, or what lessons you are learning through those experiences, let the consciousness always be centered on that one Reality — the one thing that will never fail you, that will never change, that is eternal — God, and your relationship with Him.

PARAMAHANSA.II'S
GREAT SAMADHI OF 1948

God became so very real for those of us who lived around Master not only because of the training he gave us in meditation and

spiritual living, but also through the manifes-
tations of God's infinite nature that we saw in
our Guru himself. I would like to relate one
such experience.

It was in 1948, late one afternoon. We
were busy with our duties in the office and in
the ashram at Mt. Washington, when Master
called a few of us to come to his room. We
saw from his countenance that he was very
much withdrawn in the consciousness of
God. We entered very quietly, and he mo-
tioned to us to sit on the floor, so we sat down
and began meditating.

Master was praying from the very core of
his heart to Divine Mother. He was conversing intimately with Her, pouring out to Her
all of the problems of the society that had yet
to be resolved, all the burdens that building
an organization had placed upon him. He
knew that he had not many years yet to

reside in that physical form, and much still to accomplish.

Then he moved into the adjacent room, and sat down in the large chair that was there. He asked that a mango be brought; he was going to share it with us. As he started to prepare the mango, his whole consciousness was just sucked within by God. And then we were privileged to witness something that has happened perhaps very seldom in this world.

In this *samadhi* of Master's, which lasted all night, until about eight o'clock the next morning, we saw Master conversing with God, with Divine Mother — and we heard Her using his voice to reply aloud. We heard his words to Her in his familiar voice; and when She replied, the voice was slightly changed; there was a different quality, a distinctly different timbre, in Master's voice.

As he told us, "During this *samadhi*, God is giving a very special blessing to you all, to share in my experience." Such a tremendous experience it was. During one period, Divine Mother was showing him the endless reaches of infinity. He expressed that his consciousness was flying through the cosmos, expanding to the very ends of eternity, and we heard him say to Divine Mother, "Is this the end of Infinity?"

She answered, "Yes, this is the end, and only the beginning."

Then he would traverse infinitely more distance in consciousness, and again he would say, "Is this the end?"

And again She would say, "Yes, and only the beginning."

Divine Mother related many things during that period of *samadhi* about the future of the work. Master told us that Her blessing and the blessings of Guru would always be with this special dispensation of SRF/YSS, always

available for any soul who would come to
drink of that divine nectar of God's presence.

As Master began to come out of that infinite experience, back to this world, he said
to us: "From now on, inwardly I will always
be in this consciousness; but no one will
know, no one will see."

After that period, there were many times
when Master would have very deep experiences with God. He would say to us, "You
see how my life is now. If you could just have
a glimpse of what I am experiencing within
all of the time now, you would not rest, day
or night, until you had attained that consciousness of God." In this way he would talk
to us, trying to stir us, to shake us out of the
lethargy of delusion and ignorance that
makes us think that we must spend so much
time on this body, so much time sleeping, so
much time in forgetfulness of God. "If ever
Divine Mother would show you just a little

bit of this infinite Light, Joy, Love, and freedom that I am experiencing," he would say,
"you would not rest until you had attained
that state."

DO NOT LET MAYA GO ON TRICKING YOU

If there is one thought, one message, that
I most want to leave with you, it would be
those words of Master — to shake you, as he
sought to shake us, out of any spiritual sloth-
fulness into a greater desire for God, a
greater effort to meditate deeply and to follow the ways that have been pointed out to
us by our blessed Guru and line of Gurus.

These teachings do lead to that Divine
Goal. We saw their results perfectly manifested in the life of our Guru — and in ever
so much smaller ways in our own lives, so
that we can, with the Guru, give this testi-
mony: Even a little taste of that infinite love
and joy and fulfillment that comes from God

will give you something in your life that nothing else — no human pursuit or satisfaction — can begin to give you. Try it. Make a sincere effort to experience that in your life.

Don't let delusion, or *maya*, or Satan, go on tricking you into being bound and limited to the little experiences of this human body — to physical, temporal desires and objects. Give some time to God. Out of the twenty-four hours given to us each day, can we not find even one hour for Him who created us? When you first awaken, let your thought go to God and rest in Him. Then try to carry that consciousness with you during the day. Again, the last thing at night, meditate and let your consciousness rest in Him before sleeping. If you give even one hour of the day to God in deep meditation, making sincere effort, you will see how your life changes.

He used to say: "In those little gaps of time when you are free from the necessities and responsibilities of life, don't waste time by always turning on the radio, or the television, or picking up the telephone to gossip with a friend. Use those times for God instead. Even if it is just one minute or three minutes, sit down and meditate, or just turn the consciousness within, and let the thoughts rest on God. In those few moments, feel such devotion, such love and longing for God, that the whole world recedes, and you know that the only reality is He."

The only real relationship is the relationship of your soul and Spirit — the oneness of your soul and your whole being with God. So Paramahansaji would tell us, "In those little gaps of time, if you make love to God, you will feel much more His divine response. And you will see how that love fully satisfies and fulfills your life."

Only one thing is needed, which no one else can give you; that is, your own stirring

of will and effort to practice what our Guru
has taught. I can promise you that even as
Divine Mother fulfilled and satisfied every
need — every little whim, you might
say — that ever passed through Master's consciousness, so God will do the same for you.
You have to work and carry out your responsibilities in this world. God does not intend
that you neglect those — and you do not have
to neglect them. You will find that, as I said
in the beginning, as you come closer to God
you become a more perfected and balanced
human being. You can fulfill your responsi
bilities more adequately. You can love others
more purely; and your relationships with others begin to improve. Your understanding
starts to clear, so that whatever conditions
you are faced with in life, you can reach an
unclouded perspective and see how to guide
your life through these labyrinths of experiences. God will show you the way.

As you begin to remove from your consciousness the debris of all these limitations that we have talked about tonight, it is like a fog clearing. Everything becomes clearer. Your duty to the world, to family, to humankind, to God — all begin to fall into proper perspective, and you find that you can satisfy all of these God-given responsibilities in the particular role in which He has placed you in this incarnation.

So do not let these words be simply a momentary inspiration, but make the effort to convert them into your own realization, your own attainment of the goal of this path, which is that eternal oneness, that daily, moment-by-moment communion with the reality that is God. Never let God be just a word to you. Never be content until that word has become a realization, an experience within your mind, your heart, and your soul.

PART II

The Blessings of Kriya Yoga in Everyday Life

This talk was given during one of Mrinalini Mata's six visits to India to assist with the spread of Paramahansa Yogananda's work there.

In this world of dualities and relativities, in which we find so much pain, sorrow, suffering, and turmoil, there is a definite need for a scientific knowledge of how to live. We need a science not just of bringing more material prosperity and more material "gadgets" into our lives, but a science of living. That is what humanity is missing — what is causing all of the problems and troubles in our world

today. And that is what our guru, Paramahansa Yogananda, brought to the West in his
Kriya Yoga teachings.

Through the ages, the science of living has
been given to humanity repeatedly. God's nature must be one of infinite patience, because
how else could God (of whom we speak as
the Divine Mother) go on being unendingly
loving and tolerant of Her children, patiently
reminding us: "This is My world; I created it.
I made it good, I made it beautiful. I created
you all. I made *you* good, I made *you* beautiful. I have told you in scripture, I have told
you through the voices and the examples of
the avatars and saints, again and again, what
you must do in this world to keep it beautiful,
to keep your lives in harmony with Me, so
that you bring My beauty and joy and peace
and prosperity into manifestation on this
earth — which I have created and which I

alone sustain. And yet, what have you done to this world?"

In so many ways modern culture, with a great mayic force, has tried to remove God, to dismiss Him, from a "scientific" view of the cosmos and from daily life. Yet the world will never know lasting happiness or peace or freedom from suffering so long as man denies God as the supreme Reality in this creation, which is made and sustained only by His infinite thought.

The Cause of Our Suffering

In the minds of all who suffer, there comes a time of questioning and doubt when we think: "If there is a God, why does He allow this suffering? Why has this pain come into my life? Does God hear my prayers?" And when we see millions afflicted by terrible catastrophes, wars, and disasters, we cannot help but think: "Where is God? Has He just thrown us, as a great mass of humanity, into this world of troubles and then withdrawn?"

God *is* there. He does listen, and He does respond. We see that exemplified in the lives of the saints and divine teachers. Even a person in ordinary life, who just for one moment touches that Infinite Consciousness, perhaps when some prayer has been granted, gets a glimpse and feels: "Ah, God *is* real; He does respond!" Modern shallow thinking tells us that this is "unscientific." But great ones such as our gurudeva, Paramahansa Yogananda, affirm that there is a deeper science that perfectly answers all our questions about life. This is the science of yoga.

God has not withdrawn. He created us in His image; He encased a little portion of His Infinite Consciousness in individuality and said, "Now you are a soul, and I send you into **My** world of *maya* to express a part of

My Infinite Nature" — not just as beings of pure consciousness individualized as souls, but beings encased in delimited bodies of astral life energy and then of physical matter, set amidst a vast cosmos of material objects and energies. But what happens? Man gets caught by that *maya*. Paramahansaji used to refer to *maya* as a cosmic hypnosis. In order to play the drama of creation, the Lord is powerfully suggesting to our consciousness that this world is real and we are separated from Him. Because that hypnotic suggestion is so strong, we believe it — we behold only the end result of the process of cosmic creation: the physical world and our frail physical bodies. We forget our origin in God, and our blissful, immortal divine nature, inseverably linked with Him; and that is why we begin to suffer. But there is a way out. The cosmic laws that God put into effect when He created Himself as this multitude — when He spewed out of His own Self and seemingly away from Him this infinity of individualized beings and nature — those same divine laws work in reverse. And the *application* of that knowledge is the sum and substance of the science of yoga.

RESTORING THE TRUE YOGA AS A WAY OF BALANCED SPIRITUAL LIVING

Yoga in its highest context means union: realizing that the individualized soul is, and has always been, and shall ever be, united to God. The science of yoga has been extolled by its practitioners because as soon as one begins to apply the laws that restore to conscious awareness the links by which he is eternally one with God, he also begins to draw upon the infinite qualities of God. For example, the peace of God comes as the first experience of the meditating yogi.

But through the centuries the practice of yoga became very complicated, very arcane — not something relevant to or applicable in everyday life — because some practitioners, by applying those divine laws of reversing the externalized consciousness back to God, saw that there are also "supernatural" powers and abilities that come as by-products of this process. They were working with the laws by which material creation and man's encasement in the physical body came about, and as they touched that creative power they began to develop great abilities to do both good and evil in this world, abilities not only to perceive Truth and the way to unite with God, but also psychic perceptions of the astral worlds of light out of which this physical world has evolved, and various other psychic powers. Because the ordinary man's nature, his ego, is typically invested in perpetuating himself and expressing his abilities

in this world of *maya* to which he is so at-
tached, many thought of yoga as a science of
powers, of capabilities — forgetting that yoga
is really the science of the soul: reawakening
it to the divine awareness of oneness with
God.

Yoga in this sense is very simple. It is a
way of living, a way of thinking, a way of
behaving — and more than that, a way of becoming. It is a changing of one's self. The
goal of the science of *Kriya Yoga,* which we
are speaking about tonight, is not the devel-
opment of psychic powers, nor the ability,
necessarily, to create great successes in this
world. It is to reawaken the sleeping image
of the Divine within; to realize, as the scriptures say: *Tat tvam asi,* "Thou art That" — by-
passing all that distracts or diverts you from
that all-fulfilling attainment. Guruji used to
say that when you are seeking God sincerely,
you must pass through the garden of astral

phenomena and powers and not get caught there, if you want to reach the palace where God is.

KRIYA YOGA: ITS DISPENSATION TO THE MODERN WORLD

It was in 1861, in the Himalayas near Ranikhet, that Mahavatar Babaji resurrected the lost ancient science of *Kriya Yoga* and taught it to that great saint whom we call *Yogavatar* ("Incarnation of Yoga"): Lahiri Mahasaya of Banaras, giving him permission to teach it not only to solitary ascetics who vowed themselves to complete renunciation, as in the past, but to sincere devotees with worldly responsibilities as well — "to all who humbly ask for help." Then, in 1894, one of Lahiri Mahasaya's chief disciples, Swami Sri Yukteswar, met Babaji at a *Kumbha Mela*. At that time Babaji told Sri Yukteswarji that some years later he would send him a *chela* (disciple) to train, whom he had chosen to take the *Kriya* science to the West. Later, in 1920, the Mahavatar personally told our gurudeva, Paramahansa Yogananda: "You are the one I have chosen to spread the message of *Kriya Yoga* in the West. Long ago I met your guru Yukteswar at a *Kumbha Mela;* I told him then I would send you to him for training."

Babaji foresaw that the time was coming when this world must give up its divisiveness, its sectarian hatreds, its secularism — that along with the advance of scientific knowledge and technology in this upwardly evolving era, humankind must either learn to live together or it will destroy itself. By the sending of *Kriya Yoga* to the West, the very essence of Truth — which has always been nurtured and protected in this spiritual motherland, India — would eventually spread like a great light over the whole world, gradually bringing peace, understanding, unity, harmony, and brotherhood.

KRIYA YOGA IS A PATH OF LAW AND LOVE

Guruji had first received the *Kriya* technique as a child, as both his parents were disciples of Lahiri Mahasaya. Yet later, when he was seventeen and met Swami Sri Yukteswarji, and received the *Kriya* technique from him as *diksha* — the spiritual initiation bestowed by the guru at the time of accepting a disciple — Paramahansaji said that never before had he received so much blessing, so much power, from *Kriya*.

Why? Because, as India's scriptures teach, in seeking God three things are necessary. First of all, the *chela's* effort; this is twenty-five percent of the total required for success. Secondly, the guru's blessing; this is another twenty-five percent. Great effort is required of the *chela;* but an equal amount of his

progress is due to the guru's help and inter-
cession, carrying the *chela* along the path.
And the third necessity is the grace of God,
which is fifty percent of the total. No one has
found God without going through the chan-
nel of his or her God-ordained guru; that is
the divine law. And this law is an essential
part of the science of *Kriya Yoga*.

The *Kriya Yoga* path to God is one of law and
love. Law is necessary, because if we go against
God's laws (such as expressed in the Bible's
Ten Commandments or the *yama-niyama* of
Yoga) we weave a net of delusive karma and
suffering from which it is difficult to extricate
ourselves. The supreme observance of spiritual law is *sadhana* — the way of spiritual discipline, especially practice of the *Kriya Yoga*
technique of salvation, given to the *chela* by
his guru. When the *chela* follows his *sadhana*
by faithfully and regularly doing as his guru
has taught him, he is applying law.

Along with law, the *chela* must also apply love. How sweetly Guruji used to say that God created this world, and everything in it belongs to Him. It is all His. There is only one thing that God does not have: the love of His children. It is our choice whether to love Him or to forget Him. That is part of the individuality He gave to us. Yet how painfully that forgetfulness of God keeps us enmeshed in *maya,* bound to the seeming reality of this world of duality and suffering!

Our Guru said that as he began to practice *Kriya,* he found an increasing love and longing for God awakening within him — an increasing understanding that Divine Love is the only Reality, the only Truth, in this world of duality and relativity created by that outgoing force of *maya. Kriya Yoga* is so effective, so complete, because it brings God's love — the universal power through which God draws all

souls back to reunion with Him — into operation in the devotee's life.

There is a deep metaphysical science behind this. With the vibratory power of His
mind God created the Cosmic Word, *Aum,*
the vibration that is the underlying structure
of all creation. With this great force He threw
creation — vibrations of His own One Being — out into space and gave it the capability
of infinite, individualized expression. But at
the same time God said, "I shall not let My
creation go away from Me forever. I shall not
let it roam off into eternity, to be separated
from my Infinite Consciousness. I have put
Myself in that *Aum* vibration (and thus in
each of those infinitely varied forms evolved
out of that primal Creative Vibration) as
Love — as the attracting power that counter-
acts the outgoing force of *maya,* that will pull
all creation and all My children back to re-
membrance and recognition of Me."

So Divine Love is the universal force, the magnetic power operating in creation, that keeps the universe from dissipating into chaos — the force that keeps the planets and galaxies and cosmos itself revolving in orderly cycles. It is the force of evolution, which brings about ever more highly organized life-forms, with progressive capacity to manifest higher and higher consciousness. That same magnetic power of God's love is operating in every human heart, in greater or lesser degree depending on whether one chooses to respond to that Love or ignore it.

The power of *Kriya Yoga* lies in the scientific application of these metaphysical laws. Why are we caught in this *maya*? Because the same outgoing force of creation that operates in the whole universe is also at work in our individual forms. Swept along with that force, our souls come down from awareness of oneness with God. We were created with the

ability to live in the body as divine beings — souls made in the perfect image of
God. But the moment our consciousness
leaves its throne of Spirit — in the *sahasrara*
or "thousand-petaled lotus" in the brain — and
flows down through the spinal *chakras* of life
and consciousness and outward through the
nervous system into the body, it is no longer
soul. It is now ego, *ahamkara,* identified with
the senses and body, and enveloped in delusion. It is in that state that man feels, "I am
this body. I perceive through these five
senses. I enjoy and suffer in this form. I accomplish this and that in the world; I desire
this and that from the world; I have acquired
these possessions which are mine." *I, me,
mine* — all of man's troubles start from this
body-identified state of ordinary ego
consciousness.

Kriya Yoga is that science through which
God is saying to man: "You see the way by

which going outward you have been caught in delusion; now here is the way by which going inward you can be free." *Kriya Yoga,* practiced with the blessing of Guru given at the time of *diksha* (initiation), reverses the outward-flowing creative vibratory power in his body, taking his consciousness along with his life force inward and upward through the *chakras* of the spine, through the same pathway by which it has descended into the body and senses, to be seated again in the center of his spiritual being with its infinite state of divine awareness.

THE SIMPLICITY OF THE KRIYA PATH

It is not possible in a short talk to describe all of this adequately. Tomes have been written about the intricacies of the science of yoga and how its techniques of *pranayama* (life-force control) work to take the consciousness back to God. To read and absorb them would take an entire lifetime, or more! But the *practice* of *Kriya* is very simple. The devotee does not have to understand the metaphysics involved. After all, are we running God's universe? Do the laws of physics only work when we tell them how to work? Of course not! Cosmic laws are constantly operating with or without our knowledge of their operation.

So when one practices *Kriya* — and applies not only law, as embodied in the technique, but also the other necessity I spoke of: love for God, a longing and desire for God in the heart — then automatically the profound metaphysical principles of the yoga science are called into play. By practice of the *pranayama* technique of *Kriya Yoga*, which "magnetizes" the spine, concentration becomes interiorized. And when the mind becomes concentrated upon God, and there is devotion in the heart, and one practices the very simple *Kriya* technique, automatically — without our even having to know the complicated pathways through which the *prana* revolves up and down the spine, or how the consciousness passes through the *chakras* (successively finer aspects of the creative *Aum* Vibration), or what is happening at the spiritual eye (the *kutastha*) — God's laws are working to center the consciousness within upon the altar of God-perception. One is tuning in with that great vibratory force of God's love — that magnetic force of attraction in creation and in every soul. When by devotion plus correct and long practice of *Kriya* for years if necessary — the magnetic attraction of the ingoing force becomes stronger in the devotee than the outgoing force of *maya* that has hypnotized him into thinking the physical body and world are real, then the devotee can enter at will the state of interiorized God-communion.

THE STILLNESS AFTER KRIYA:
REAL WORSHIP OF THE DIVINE

The Bible teaches, "Be still and know that I am God." In India the scriptures have spoken of the Divine Beloved One: "I am that stillness beyond all motion, beyond all vibration, beyond all form." When the devotee becomes deeply still and concentrated, he enters those states spoken of by Patanjali in the *Yoga Sutras* as *pratyahara* and then *dharana,* wherein the mind is no longer conscious of the body nor anything in the external environment — freed from all obstacles of distraction. And when one takes that concentrated interiorized attention and puts it fully upon God, that is the state Patanjali called *dhyana,* real meditation. As though by a great magnet, the consciousness has been drawn within so that, at least momentarily, we rise above ego and forget the body. In that stillness, we begin to feel the Divine One — and to realize that we have never for an instant been separated from Spirit.

In that state, God's first expression to us is usually peace, a peace "which surpasseth all understanding," a peace that is utterly soothing — not a negative state of mental blankness, but one of keen awareness and perception. And to the devotee who goes on calling to God with the whole being while in that state of peace and stillness, the Lord will respond in whatever form or aspect is nearest and dearest to that devotee's heart and need and longing. As Lord Krishna said in the Gita, "In whatever way a devotee worships Me, in that way do I come to him."

We cannot truly worship God in external ceremony, or chanting, or anything which keeps our attention outward. The real *puja*, the real *yajna* (sacrifice or performance of holy rite), is the science of *Kriya Yoga* wherein the devotee makes the one offering that truly touches the Divine Heart: "Lord, into the fire of Spirit which I perceive within myself, I cast forever all of my egoity, all of my meanness, all of my selfishness, all of my personal desires and ambitions, all of my bad habits and flaws, to be burned forever in the fire of divine awakening of your Spirit, which is living right within me." That is the true worship of God, the true *puja*, which takes place within.

How to Be Anchored in God While Active in the World

Perhaps I can convey to you most aptly the effect of this science of *Kriya Yoga* by giving examples of what it has done in the lives of others. *Kriya Yoga*, as we saw it manifested in the life of our Gurudeva over so many years, made him always internally anchored in divine consciousness. Yet he was very active in this world for God and humanity, exemplifying the Lord's ideal in the Bhagavad Gita of meditation plus right activity. The Lord is saying, "I put you children here. You must be My instruments, My divine agents, to make this world a better place, to love and help one another. Your first duty is to seek your own salvation; but having begun to taste of the sweetness of My Being, then share that with all. Uplift your suffering brothers and sisters — those in darkness, delusion and ignorance — that they no longer make the mistakes that have caused their suffering."

That was the whole of Guruji's life: internally a *bhakta* of all-surrendering devotion, yet outwardly a *karma yogi*, working tirelessly for all in this world — so that you and I and countless souls in all lands would hear this message and know there is a way not just to know *about* God, but actually to commune with Him.

Kriya Yoga enables us to serve with far more than mere words. As exemplified by Guruji, this science shows that when we touch the infinite being of God in the stillness of meditation, something of that Divinity becomes a part of us. When meditation is over and we return to our outer roles in this world, we find we have brought with us some of God's divine qualities. Having borrowed from His wisdom, we are better able to grasp the meaning of life, to understand others, to see through our own problems in life and to find the right solutions. Having absorbed from the love of God, we become able to forgive those who wrong us. Guruji used to say that evil must be resisted in this world; one should not cooperate with or support any evil or wrongdoing that breaks God's divine laws. But, he said, while you resist the wrongdoing, love and forgive the wrongdoer, realizing that he is a child of God in delusion. Think what unity, what a fellow-feeling of brotherhood and harmony there would be if we could all share a little bit of that divine love. The true *Kriya Yogi* is able to do that — and also to borrow from the other divine qualities of God; His infinite peace and calmness, for example. The *Kriya Yogi* is able, as Guruji so beautifully expressed, "to stand unshaken amidst the crash of breaking worlds."

Only God is unchanging. Everything in His externalized creation that we perceive and experience is constantly changing. Change frightens us and irritates us; but the *Kriya Yogi*, anchored in That which is changeless, is able to go through his duties and responsibilities in life, maintaining the peace and calmness that help him to better cope with his problems and troubles. And because he can cope with his own, he can better help others with theirs.

THE BLESSINGS OF KRIYA IN THE LIVES OF PARAMAHANSAJI'S DISCIPLES

We saw the effects of *Kriya Yoga* not only in the life of our divine Gurudeva, but also in his spiritual successors. Rajarsi Janakananda was one of the great material successes in the West. He was the president of one of the largest underwriting insurance corporations in the United States, and owned numerous other business concerns. Before meeting Gurudeva, in 1932, though, his health and well-being had been shattered by materiality and nervousness. At their first meeting, Gurudeva gave him the *diksha* of *Kriya Yoga*, and with his very first practice Rajarsi entered *samadhi*. Gurudeva said he could do this because he had been a yogi in past lives and had already gathered much good karma. But he did not leave the world. Guruji said that Rajarsi's role, even as Lahiri Mahasaya in India had demonstrated, was to be in the world but not of it: to show the effect that *Kriya* can have in those who carry worldly responsibilities as householders.

Whenever he could find time from his duties in Kansas City, he would come to Guruji's ashram in Encinitas by the Pacific Ocean. There we would see Rajarsi for hours sitting out under the sun in the hottest weather, or sometimes sitting there when it would start to rain, just lost in *samadhi*. He loved to swim out in the ocean, go into *matsyasana* — the "fish pose" in which one is lying back in the lotus posture — and, like a cork, float on the waves in *samadhi*. For hours at a time we would see him out there. And he carried that inner communion into all of his duties.*

---

* Rajarsi Janakananda was a beloved and exalted disciple of Paramahansa Yogananda, and his first spiritual successor as president of Self-Realization Fellowship. He served in that position from 1952 until his passing in 1955.

During those years we also saw that Gurudeva had singled out Sri Daya Mata, who had come to him in 1931 when only seventeen years old. He said that up until that time he was thinking, "Lord, where are those *chela*s in whom I can truly plant this work, who will carry it on and keep it pure, as I promised my Guru?" He said that when Daya Mataji first came, "I saw she was the one that God had chosen." She has told us that Guruji once said to her, "If you practice nothing but *Kriya* in this life, you will reach the Goal." And through her utter dedication to Guru and practice of his *Kriya Yoga* teachings, how beautifully her life and divine love have touched thousands all over the world throughout her decades of leading his work.*

---

* Sri Daya Mata passed away on November 30, 2010, after serving as president of SRF/YSS for more than 55 years.

KRIYA YOGA'S BLESSING FOR THE WORLD

Such are the blessings of *Kriya Yoga*. It transforms all who truly practice into children of the beloved Divine Mother: divine ones who are able to share with all humanity peace, understanding, unconditional love. God doesn't intend that the world go on forgetting Him, with only a few saints coming now and then as exceptions. Through the message of *Kriya Yoga* given by our Gurudeva and *Paramgurus,* God is saying, "You are all divine children. It is your sacred privilege and duty to follow a science of the soul, to regain the realization of your oneness with Me." By contacting God in meditation, each one of you must bring Him into your own life, your own being, your own consciousness, so that *you* become changed — so that darkness is banished from your own consciousness. If the electricity goes off, it is not enough if only one or two in this large auditorium lights a match. But if everyone lights a little match, the whole room becomes illumined. So it is, when the science of *Kriya Yoga* will catch fire in many hearts around this world, its light will dispel discouragement and delusion everywhere.

ABOUT THE AUTHOR

Sri Mrinalini Mata, one of those personally trained and chosen by Paramahansa Yogananda to carry on the aims of his society after his passing, has been president and spiritual head of Self-Realization Fellowship/Yogoda Satsanga Society of India since 2011. She has dedicated more than 60 years to self-lessly serving Paramahansa Yogananda's work.

It was in 1945, at the Self-Realization Fellowship Temple in San Diego, that the future Mrinalini Mata first met Paramahansa Yogananda. She was then fourteen years old. Just a few months later, her desire to dedicate her life to seeking and serving God found fulfillment when, with her parents' permission, she entered Sri Yogananda's ashram in Encinitas, California, as a nun of the Self-Realization Order.

Through daily association during the years that followed (up until the time of the Guru's passing in 1952), Paramahansaji devoted close attention to the spiritual training of this young nun. (She also completed her formal education in the local schools.) From the very beginning of her life in the ashram, he recognized and spoke openly to the other disciples about her future role, and personally trained her to prepare his writings and talks for publication after his passing.

Mrinalini Mata (whose name refers to the lotus flower, traditionally regarded in India as a symbol of purity and spiritual unfoldment) has served for many years as editor-in-chief of Self-Realization Fellowship books, lessons, and periodicals. Among the works that have been published as a result of her efforts are Paramahansa Yogananda's masterful commentary on the four Gospels (entitled *The Second Coming of Christ: The Resurrection of the Christ Within You*); his critically acclaimed translation and commentary on the Bhagavad Gita (*God Talks With Arjuna*); several volumes of his poetry and inspirational writings; and three lengthy anthologies of his collected talks and essays.

OTHER BOOKS AND RECORDINGS
BY SRI MRINALINI MATA

Books

The Guru-Disciple Relationship
(How-to-Live Booklet)

CDs

Living in Attunement With the Divine

Look Always to the Light

The Guru: Messenger of Truth

If You Would Know the Guru:
Remembrances of Life With Paramahansa Yogananda

The Interior Life

The Yoga Sadhana That Brings God's Love and Bliss

DVDs

In His Presence: Remembrances of Life With
Paramahansa Yogananda

Portal to the Inner Light: Official Release of
Paramahansa Yogananda's *The Second Coming of
Christ: The Resurrection of the Christ Within You*

Be Messengers of God's Light and Love

The Second Coming of Christ: Making of a Scripture—
Reminiscences by Sri Daya Mata and Sri Mrinalini
Mata

Available online at www.yogananda-srf.org

About Paramahansa Yogananda

Paramahansa Yogananda (1893–1952) is widely regarded as one of the preeminent spiritual figures of our time. Born in northern India, he came to the United States in 1920, where he taught India's ancient science of meditation and the art of balanced spiritual living for more than thirty years. Through his acclaimed life story, *Autobiography of a Yogi,* and his numerous other books, Paramahansa Yogananda has introduced millions of readers to the perennial wisdom of the East. Today his spiritual and humanitarian work is carried on by Self-Realization Fellowship, the international society he founded in 1920 to disseminate his teachings worldwide.

BOOKS BY PARAMAHANSA YOGANANDA

Available at bookstores
or online at www.yogananda-srf.org

Autobiography of a Yogi

Autobiography of a Yogi *(Audiobook, read by Sir Ben Kingsley)*

God Talks With Arjuna: The Bhagavad Gita (A New Translation and Commentary)

The Second Coming of Christ: The Resurrection of the Christ Within You (A Revelatory Commentary on the Original Teachings of Jesus)

The Collected Talks and Essays
    Volume I: Man's Eternal Quest
    Volume II: The Divine Romance
    Volume III: Journey to Self-realization

Wine of the Mystic: The Rubaiyat of Omar Khayyam— A Spiritual Interpretation

The Yoga of Jesus

The Yoga of the Bhagavad Gita

The Science of Religion

Whispers from Eternity

Songs of the Soul

Sayings of Paramahansa Yogananda

Scientific Healing Affirmations

Where There Is Light: Insight and Inspiration for Meeting Life's Challenges

In the Sanctuary of the Soul: A Guide to Effective
    Prayer
Inner Peace: How to Be Calmly Active and Actively Calm
How You Can Talk With God
Metaphysical Meditations
The Law of Success
Cosmic Chants

*A complete catalog of books and audio/video recordings — includ-
ing rare archival recordings of Paramahansa Yogananda — is
available on request or online at www.yogananda-srf.org.*

SELF-REALIZATION FELLOWSHIP LESSONS

The scientific techniques of meditation taught by
Paramahansa Yogananda, including *Kriya Yoga* — as well as
his guidance on all aspects of balanced spiritual living — are
presented in the *Self-Realization Fellowship Lessons.* For further information, please ask for the free introductory
booklet, *Undreamed-of Possibilities.*

SELF-REALIZATION FELLOWSHIP
3880 San Rafael Avenue • Los Angeles, CA 90065-3219
Tel *(323) 225-2471* • Fax *(323) 225-5088*
www.yogananda-srf.org